THE PEOPLE OF INDIA

THE PEOPLE OF INDIA

MORTIMER MENPES

AND

G. E. MITTON

GYAN

Published by

Gyan Publishing House
5, Ansari Road
Daryaganj, New Delhi-110002
Phone: 011-47034999, 9811692060
E-mail: books@gyanbooks.com

Distribution Network
gyanbooks.com
India, USA, Canada, UK, Australia

ISBN: 978-93-7014-910-6 (HB)

First Published, 1910

2nd Impression 2025

Printed at: Gyan Press, Delhi.

THE PEOPLE OF INDIA

Author: MORTIMER MENPES AND G. E. MITTON

THE PEOPLE OF INDIA

THE PEOPLE OF INDIA

PAINTED BY

MORTIMER MENPES

WITH INTRODUCTION BY

G. E. MITTON

1910

LIST OF ILLUSTRATIONS IN COLOUR

THE PEOPLE OF INDIA

OF the large minority of English people who have not visited India, it is safe to say that there are few who do not feel as if they had, so strong is their familiarity with the mighty peninsula by reason of the pictures and descriptions so freely scattered among us. Yet the absurdity of this vague and nebulous "knowledge" is most clearly demonstrated directly there arises any discussion concerning the great races of India. A murmur of Sikhs, Hindus, and possibly Ghoorkas, will be all that most people can produce under such pressure, and yet this probably represents, fairly enough, all that they know of the "variegated jumble of races and peoples, castes and creeds, that make up the population of India," to use the words of the well-equipped and able writer, who, in 1910, published a series of articles on India in *The Times*.

Not even the most learned ethnologist can say definitely what is the exact ancestry of the fine war-like men who supply the material for some of our best regiments in India, still less can they sort out into its true elements the composite ancestry of the mass of the people. We do know, however, that the highest caste of Hindus, the proud Brahmans, and the splendid men who form the aristocracy of the Rajputs, are of pure Aryan blood, having kept themselves distinct and refused to intermarry with other classes. In the striking faces of some of these men the influence of centuries of command is clearly stamped, and their physiognomy is in marked contrast to the lower classes, of Madrassis, for example, whose round faces and thick noses betray traces of negro origin, possibly derived from ancestors who came over from Arabia in the successive waves of Mohammedan incursions. The vast mass of the people are of extremely mixed blood, and Scythians, Persians, Aryans, etc., have alike contributed to their making; the traits of one or another standing out predominantly in members of the same family.

Of the aborigines, some have sunk into the general mass, but others still preserve their characteristics, living in caves and hill-corners, generally in a degraded state. Among these may be reckoned the Bhils, the Gonds, the Kols, the Nairs, and many another tribe, now of little importance except ethnographically.

Perhaps the classification most easily understood is that of religion, which, to some extent, though very roughly, follows the lines of race cleavage. The Hindus, who form by far the largest proportion of the total population, are naturally the best known; as already indicated, Hinduism in some form was brought in by the Aryan invasion. To this religion most of the native Princes ruling independent States belong. The Hindus are to the Mohammedans as about three to one.

The Mohammedans, the next in order numerically, can claim the Nizam of Hyderabad, who rules the largest independent State, as belonging to their religion. The Mohammedans swept in upon the Aryans in waves, and though stubbornly resisted succeeded in establishing a dynasty which lasted for many hundreds of years. To the Mohammedan Moguls belong the proudest names in Indian history—those of Baber, Akbar and Aurungzebe, father, grandson, and great-grandson. At the present time the Mohammedans dread the power of the Hindus, who so far outnumber them, and it is certain that were ever British rule to be withdrawn from India, the Hindus would make a desperate attempt to drive their Mohammedan fellow-countrymen into the sea, and thus to sweep the country clear of them.

The Buddhists are the next most important in number, and though the Buddhists are only as one in twenty to the Mohammedans, they are not in the same position, because they are segregated to a great extent; the mass of the Buddhists being the Shans and Burmans of Burma, or Further India, and some, of a slightly different type, being found in the independent States of Sikkim and Bhutan; they are not scattered throughout India. The Sikhs are a mere handful in number, about half as many as the Buddhists; the Jains and

Parsees also count but little in a population numbered in millions.

After religion there is the evidence of language to be considered. Even those who have lived in the country would probably consider that "Hindustanee" forms a good general answer as to an Indian national language; it is, of course, the *lingua franca*, but the number of separate languages is legion. To quote the same writer already referred to, "there is a greater diversity of races, languages, social customs, physical conditions, etc., between the different provinces of India than is often to be found between the different countries of Europe." It is difficult, indeed, to regard the mighty peninsula as if it were a congeries of European countries, with Russian, German, English, French, and Italian straitly defining the boundaries of the nations; yet the Latin languages, French, Italian, and Spanish, are all closely akin, and German, English, and the Danish tongues have a common origin. Certainly not farther apart are these from one another than the tongues of the races of India. Here are a few: Marathi, Gujerati, Sindhi, Kanarese, Tamil, Telugu, Bengali, Bihari, Assamese, Punjabi, to say nothing of Burmese. Some of these languages are allied, as Tamil and Telugu, but they are more than mere variations of dialect, having split off so far back that they may fairly be classed as languages by themselves. As for the oldest Aryan tongue, the Sanscrit, this is preserved in the sacred writings, but has long ceased to be understandable by any but the priestly caste.

To come now to a few of the outstanding races. Of all those in India, the Rajputs are the proudest. The Maharaja of Udaipur is the premier prince of all the Rajputs, and he claims a descent which reaches back into the mythical ages—in fact, it is supposed to begin with the sun and moon! His insignia shows a golden sun rayed on a huge disc of black ostrich feathers, and is worshipped by all Hindus. Out of the nineteen States of Rajputana, sixteen are ruled by hereditary Rajput chiefs, and the rulers of Mysore, Cochin, and Travancore also claim Rajput blood. The small statured race of Ghoorkas claim also to be Rajputs, though showing marked characteristics of their own. The Maharaja of Kashmir is, oddly enough, a Rajput, though his subjects are of very mixed race and religion. The distinguishing characteristic of the Rajputs is their virility; they are fighters, and their strong noses and bushy beards seem to proclaim the fact.

Though the Sikhs are bound together by religion, and not by race, yet they formed a kingdom of their own in the Punjab, with Lahore as capital. Their sacred city is Amritsar. The Sikh religion embraces such tenets as the abolition of caste, the unity of the Godhead, and purity of life; their women are free, and the results of the religion, which to them is an active force in daily life, is seen in their conduct, for a finer, sterner set of men is found nowhere in India. They have been likened to Cromwell's "Ironsides." They are magnificent fighters, and the veriest tyro in Indian history knows of the two Sikh wars which ended in the annexation of the Punjab. Though the Mutiny occurred but eight years after this annexation, the Sikhs were determinedly loyal to their new rulers, and proved a splendid defence in the hour of need. They not only remained loyal themselves, but were able to send help to the rest of the country in the throes of revolution. The Sikh fashion is to wear a long, flowing, untrimmed beard, which gives refinement to the face, and their keen, sharp features are also usually refined, while the prevailing expression of their faces is that endorsed by experience—they are to be trusted. Sikh chiefs rule in Patiala, Nabha, and Kapurthala. The name of the Maharaja of Patiala is well known in England, where his sporting instincts and high code have won him many friends. The inhabitants of the native State of Jind in the Punjab are mixed Hindus and Sikhs.

The whole question of the native Prince-rulers of India is most interesting. There are, in all, close upon 700 native States enfolded in British territory, and occupying a position unique in the world. They vary in size from the huge domain of the Nizam, almost as large as the United Kingdom, down to small estates like those held by English country gentlemen; of them all, only about 200 are worth taking into account, the others being mere chieftainships. The Prince-rulers cannot make war or peace upon their own initiative; their protection is ensured by the British Empire, but in return for the security they enjoy they are expected to keep their territories in order and to deal justly with their people. The unanimity with which these native rulers have declared themselves on the side of the governing authority in the late unrest is most remarkable. It may be thought that they have done this with an eye to their own interests, or under coercion. The former contention may be true, but the fact they do see it is to their own interests and the interests of their country to back up British rule is the whole point, and as for coercion, what there is runs the other way, for it must have required considerable courage for an Oriential to speak out boldly and unequivocably, especially when his doing so might be cast up against him as a dereliction from loyalty to his own people. The single exception to the emphatic endorsement of British policy came from the Gaekwar of Baroda, whose language was not ardent, but rather cool.

No more brilliant idea was ever conceived than that of making a corps for ruling chiefs and nobles alone, and when Lord Curzon formed the Imperial Cadet Corps he opened out a fine training-ground for many a native Prince who inherited with the daring blood of his ancestors an aptitude for soldiering which, up till then, he had been unable to gratify in any way.

The race of the Mahrattas is another of which notice must be taken in even the most cursory survey of the peoples of India. The Maharaja of Kohlapur claims descent from the great Shivaj, the cruel marauder whose name is held in such unspeakable veneration among the Hindus; he is the only ruling Mahratta chief thus distinguished. The Mahrattas are a virile race, wiry rather than sturdy; they came in upon the ruins of the Mogul Empire and carved for themselves kingdoms, until they in turn had to yield to the British. Bombay was obtained in great part by annexations from them, and their language, Marathi, which has an abundant popular literature, is one of the spoken languages in the province.

The tribes of the extreme north, to be found in Kashmir and among the high hill-passes leading over into Tibet, are very different in physique and countenance from the men of the richer plains. Accustomed to no prodigality of nature, but to a stony land, over which icy blizzards sweep with frequency, they have learnt neither to expect to receive, nor to give; every stranger sighted is potentially an enemy. Their one consolation lies in the yaks, which, rough as the men themselves, brave extreme cold with hardihood, and are not only beasts of burden, but supply their masters with milk, clothing and fuel. Yaks are to the Kashmiris as camels to the dwellers in the desert, and a man's wealth is reckoned by the number of them he owns. One of the greatest contrasts to be found anywhere in India is that between these lean, slow-witted, enduring men, and the well-fed, glib Bengali of the rich river plains around Calcutta. Of all the types familiar to Europeans the Bengali is the best known. These men cannot be called a race in the same way that the Rajputs and Mahrattas are races; they are of mixed origin, Aryan, Mongolian, Dravidian, and are the result of many intermarriages. Yet in recent years the Bengalis have begun to claim recognition as a "nation," and it was for this reason that the partition of Bengal, decided upon for administrative convenience, aroused so much bitterness. The chief characteristic of the Bengali is his amazing appetite for knowledge; he literally sucks it in, and though his discontent is often due to mental indigestion, brought on by a superficial acquaintance with too vast an area of thought, yet when it is considered that all his work is done in a foreign language, his success and application are astounding. He has not the virility of the purer races—in fact, he is often a bit of a coward—but he is quick-witted, imaginative, impulsive, and his flow of language has long been a by-word. As a babu, or Government clerk, the Bengali is at his best, for though too easily led, apt to be inflated by an undue sense of his own importance, and utterly lacking in initiative, yet he is supple and keen, has a marvellous memory and a pigeon-hole mind. Anyone who can pass an examination and get into Government service is considered a made man for life. Below the babus are the large class of craftsmen, including some of the finest workers in the world. The crafts descend from father to son: a man who is a weaver will have had weaver forbears, and he who keeps a shop will have descended from a shop-keeping race; the trades run in families in a way unknown among our own people.

No account, however superficial, of the races of the Indian Empire would be complete without some reference to the Shans and Burmese, both as representatives of the Buddhist section of the population and as the outstanding types of that Indo-Chinese race which forms a link between the Indians on the one side and the Chinese on the other. Probably no people attracted more attention at the Durbar—that marvellous assemblage of the peoples of India—than the Shans, who appeared in great force. Their clean-shaven, round ruddy faces, generally marked by smiling contentment, stood out amidst the Hindus. The Shans are of a fairer skin than Indians, approximating more to the yellow-skinned natives of China, and no one ever sees a Shan with a beard. They are of medium height and very stoutly built, thus again contrasting with the slimmer Hindus. They follow the Burmese custom of tattooing the legs of the males from the knees above the thighs, which gives the appearance of a pair of tight knee-breeches. In Buddhism no caste is recognized, and the women are as free as the men. The result is seen in the generally happy outlook on life, for the freedom of religion shows itself in the very expression of the races who follow it.

No word has yet been said as to the women of India, and for the women the deepest lines of cleavage undoubtedly run in religion, far more than is the case even with the men. The custom of strict seclusion of womankind practised by the Mohammedans was adopted by the Hindus, and now, except in the lowest classes of all, the hewers of wood and drawers of water, the women are kept strictly "purdah"—it is an offence even to mention a man's wife. In spite of all the British Government can do to prevent it, the life of a Hindu widow, child though she may be, is a bitter one. In rural districts women are of necessity more free than in the towns, though the "sari," the cloak of disguise, often much more a metaphorical than an actual protection, is never thrown aside, and an Indian woman seen without her "sari" would be marked as belonging to one particular class. But it is the view of a woman's position in a future life far more than any actual custom in the present world which contributes to her degradation; while women are supposed to have no souls, or to hang on to a chance of heaven by their husbands, or only to arrive there after having passed through the transmigration of manhood, it is small wonder that the women, who themselves believe these things, should submit to the contempt of the superior being man. To the

Hindu, marriage is a sacred duty, for neither man nor woman can worship apart, and therefore no religious life is possible to the unmarried. Among the Buddhists there is no such thing as a bachelor or spinster; marriage is as inevitable as death. Holding these views deeply embedded in their minds, small wonder is it that unmarried English ladies who go about freely are stumbling-blocks to the native women. Still more perplexing is it to the Hindu or Mohammedan to see English ladies driving freely about with and chatting familiarly to their men acquaintances. Such conduct seems infamous, and if Eastern seclusion appears to Western ideas pitiable, no less pitiable to the Eastern mind is the apparent abandonment of our womenkind. The Parsees allow their women much freedom, and in Burma women are practically on an equality with men, doing business and making bargains, and they often prove themselves the better halves in very truth.

A SOLDIER OF THE MAHARAJA OF SIKKIM

A RAJPUT OF RAJGARH

A RETAINER FROM RAJGARH

A HAWKSMAN OF RAJGARH

A KASHMIRI PUNDAT

A SIKH SPEAR-BEARER

A SIKH WARRIOR

SPEAR-BEARER FROM JIND

A RETAINER FROM JIND

OF THE IMPERIAL CADET CORPS

AN ARMED RETAINER OF THE BOMBAY CHIEFS

HORSEMAN FROM BOMBAY

A HINDU HILL-SHEPHERD OF KASHMIR

A KASHMIRI SOLDIER

A TAILOR

A SEED STALL, DELHI

LATE AFTERNOON

WATER-CARRIERS AT NUTHA

HINDU WOMAN

A SOLDIER OF HIS HIGHNESS
DOGRA SOWAR

AN ELEPHANT AND RETAINERS FROM BIKANIR

A NATIVE BULLOCK-CART, BIKANIR

A FORMIDABLE WARRIOR OF REWA

A RETAINER OF THE MAHARAJA OF CUTCH

A RETAINER FROM CUTCH

A STANDARD-BEARER OF CUTCH

A NATIVE BRIDE

MARKET-WOMEN OF AJMERE

A SINGING-GIRL

A RETAINER FROM CENTRAL INDIA

NAUTCH GIRLS